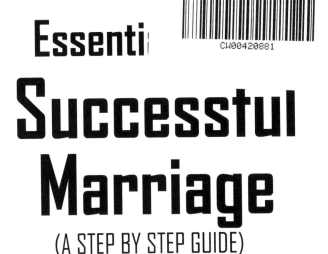

Essenti Successful Marriage
(A STEP BY STEP GUIDE)

Abiola Soremekun

All RIGHTS RESERVED

ISBN: 9798663230629

DEDICATION

This book is dedicated to God, the Author of life, for without His grace, I would not be where I am today,

To my husband; Okikiolu, thank you so much for your support and for being a loving and a wonderful husband,

To my children; Tifeoluwani and Afareayo; for being my biggest cheerleaders,

To my mother, a jewel of inestimable value...

Thank you and love you all.

TABLE OF CONTENTS

ABOUT THE AUTHOR

Abiola Soremekun is a passionate aspiring Author, Speaker, Trainer, Life Coach and Mentor. She hails from the South West part of Nigeria but lives in Lagos. She has a passion for writing and imparting knowledge to help people live their best lives!

Abiola holds a Master's Degree in Business Administration, and a Diploma in Strategic Management and Leadership from the University of Leicester, United Kingdom as well as B.Sc. in Industrial Chemistry from the University of Lagos, Nigeria. She also holds a Diploma in Theology and more than a dozen certifications from participation in various Training programmes.

Abiola works in the Oil and Gas industry and she is a member of the Nigerian Association of Petroleum Explorationists (NAPE), John Maxwell Team (JMT); the United States of America, Chartered Management Institute (CMI); the United Kingdom, and Nigerian Institute of Training and Development (NITAD).

v

When she isn't working or writing, Abiola enjoys writing, reading, travelling, networking and listening to music. She is infinitely dedicated and objective-driven and always strives to make a positive impact in people's lives. She firmly believes that "Knowledge is Power" and with her extensive knowledge, she aims to empower others through everything she does. She is married to Okiki Soremekun and they are blessed with children.

FOREWORD

Why am I writing this book? My experience from childhood to adulthood made me realize the importance of a successful marriage and its significant impact on children. The most important decision after salvation is the choice of a spouse in the life of any individual. Every man born of a woman has a God-given destiny and purpose. Marriage can either progress this destiny, alter or even end it, likewise that of children in the marriage. There have been countless stories of children whose destinies were altered through troubled marriages and spouses who have passed on in the same fate.

This is not to say that children from single parents do not do well in life, afterall I'm a living testimony of such, however I believe God does have a purpose for creating the marriage institution with blessings of fruitfulness and instructions on how to nurture the fruit! The Bible says to train up a child in the way that he should go and when he is old he will not depart from it. I believe the instruction is for parents since God knows that their roles in training and nurturing is very significant as it would have a positive impact on that child.

I am the third of five children by my mother and eleven by my father. My late father was a Muslim and had five wives of which my mother is the first. I grew up with lots of unpleasant memories due to constant hostility, bickering, and envy within the family and with external members of the family. My parents eventually separated while I was in primary school, and my mother had to enroll me and my two older siblings into a school with boarding facilities. She did this not out of a lack of love and care for her children, but she needed to do so, to enable her to leave her teaching profession and venture into business to make ends meet.

Growing up through secondary and tertiary institutions was tough and financially challenging, and the painful part was that; my father was rich and comfortable, but we were unable to benefit from him financially, simply because we were victims of circumstance! I remember then as a child, making a silent vow, neither to be in the situation I went through as a child nor allow my children to pass through the same. Eventually, I finished school, secured a job, and moved on in life. However, I couldn't help but wonder how it might have been if things were different...

The first five years of marriage are the foundation and bonding time between couples. My purpose for this book is to help couples pass through this important phase of marriage and beyond into a "happily-ever-after" marriage!

INTRODUCTION

Therefore shall a man leave his father and his mother, and shall cleave unto his wife: and they shall be one flesh. Genesis 2:24.

Now I'm married, what next? I want to believe many newly married couples would at one time have uttered this phrase. Almost every person who wish to marry dream about marriage, more often than not, they have expectations of a beautiful wedding and a blissful marriage with no issues or challenges. These dreams are not bad in itself; rather it is the expectation of a "happily-ever-after" marriage without much effort on their part to achieve their desire. Friends, I wish to inform you today that it is possible to have a "happily-ever-after-marriage, if and only if, you are ready to allow God into your home and make the necessary efforts and adjustments to make it work. At this point, I want you to drop whatever misconception or baggage that you may have about marriage and get ready to take a ride with me into your "happily-ever-after" home!

Marriage is not just about day dreaming; that man or woman whom you think is a hero or an angel, will soon turn out to be human with weaknesses, mistakes, and flaws as everyone else. However, if you are not quick to understand this and make the necessary adjustments to live with your supposed hero or angel, then the shock of reality that will hit you may bring such disappointment that may be difficult to overcome.

Marriage is real, and we have to be realistic in our approach to it. It is a coming together of a man and a woman with different backgrounds, training, experience, knowledge, strengths, weaknesses, beliefs, values, likes, and dislikes. You can never tell if your spouse snores when he or she is sleeping until you are married. And if you come to find out that your spouse snores on your wedding night, what will you do? Quit or adjust? What will you do if you have a spendthrift as a wife or husband? What will you do if you have a spouse who has an offensive body odor, while you are the type who gets irritated with smell? What if your man turns out to be a person who does not listen and considers your own opinion? Are you going to quit or adjust until you find a common ground? Let us come to terms with the truth of the matter; "all that glitters is not gold." There is a lot of dross that needs to be removed from a substance before the beauty is revealed. This, of course, takes a lot of patience and adjustments.

We live in a world where social-economic variables are unpredictable. The market can be up this morning, and by evening, it is down. Money can be good this morning and thereafter, before the close of a business drop in value, or that particular currency crumbles against other currencies. If you are the type one who does not understand the working and operation of money, and are not disciplined enough to know how to make the necessary adjustment as events unfold in the market economy, you may be thrown off balance when your spouse starts to experience financial challenges and as a result request a cut in expenses. The truth of the matter friends, is that your marriage is what you make of it. It can never and will never make itself. You will experience many issues in the course of the marriage, the moment the feasting and the jubilation of the wedding are over.

It is said that the first five years of marriage are very crucial as it is the bonding stage. With this in mind, I will proceed to share with you seven essentials of marriage that will help you jump start a "happily-ever-after" marriage within the first few weeks, months, and years of your marriage. There are of course other principles that apply to marriages, however, for this book, we shall dwell on these seven essentials namely Communication, Trust, Finance, Romance, Commitment, Love and Prayer.

So are you ready to make the unavoidable adjustments that will make your marriage work?

CHAPTER ONE
COMMUNICATION

Can two walk together, except they be agreed? Amos 3:3.

What is Communication?

Communication is defined as the act of using words, sounds, signs or behaviors to express or exchange information, ideas, thoughts, and feelings. The 1828 Webster's dictionary also defines communication as interaction by words, letters or messages. From the marriage point of view, communication harmonizes a husband and wife together in thought and actions as the sexual act does to their bodies. Every marriage is consummated by the sexual act, which binds and bonds the two together as one. The aim, goal, and purpose of communication is a fusing together of thoughts, likes, and attitudes through words and actions.

Let me reiterate here that communication, that is, effective communication harmonizes the thoughts and attitudes of a husband and wife together.

Without harmonization in the thought, action, and talk, the marriage will be strained, even if there is a harmonization of the body in the place of the sexual act. To have a blissful marriage, communication and not just sex alone must be worked at, until unity and harmony are achieved on the long run. Just imagined how much peace and understanding you would have in your home if you and your spouse are locked together in thoughts and understanding. Imagine that your spouse can predict what you will say or do in his place if you were to stand in or act for him or her. This is harmony achieved through effective communication.

I believe that every sincere individual who knows and understands the power of oneness in marriage deeply appreciates the place of this kind of communication. But believe me, it does not come cheap. You have to work at getting through to it. You have to consciously tell yourself that for my marriage to succeed, I must work at effective communication; I must work at harmonizing my thoughts, inactions, and actions with that of my spouse. And you must also be ready to get up and get going if you fail in an attempt to do this. Or should I tell you ahead of time that you are going to fail in your first attempts at this? Don't be surprised that you may have to put in about two or more years into working at this kind of communication before you ever come close to it. I am not trying to create fear in your mind; I am just being realistic, communication is interaction through words, letters and messages, it takes real work and time. But in the long run, the result is worthwhile if you keep at it and get it done. Wouldn't you rather work at something of this nature that will bring peace into your home?

Why Communication?
Have you heard this affirmation; "communication is the bedrock of every relationship"? I guess you must have. But the question is: "why is that affirmation that assertive"! Bedrock is something that is solidly fundamental, a strong base on which other things can be built on or derived. Do you know that the act of lovemaking is driven by communication? The body language of couples must be understood in the act for effective release, and that is communication too!

So, why communication in marriage? The answer is: communication is the live wire that makes the marriage work. Without it, the marriage will ultimately fail if it has not already failed. If that is the truth, how is it that most spouses never spend the time, resources and energy to learn the art of effective communication in their home? Well, I believe the answer is that too many of us overlook it by concentrating on other things that are not as important as this one, thinking that communication will automatically take its place. No sir and no ma! There is nothing automatic in your marriage; you get what you work for, and keep what you consistently worked at.

The earth needs the sun to survive, otherwise, the world's vegetation will become history, likewise, the marriage needs communication to succeed otherwise it might all just be history or pretense in the long run. I say this because I have seen a lot of couples who paint a picture of "all is well" but in the actual, nothing is well at all. A woman can pretend before the public just so that the husband will not be offended, but she cannot pretend at home. What is not is not, even though we pretend it is.

Let me tell you this; 60% of problems in marriage will be resolved if couples learn to communicate and harmonize in thoughts and actions. So to make your marriage work, you and your spouse must find effective ways of communicating, giving and receiving expressions at all times. Trust will be built if you learn how to communicate with your spouse efficiently. Money issue will be handled and treated effectively if you know how and when to communicate with your spouse. To this end, communication is key to having a blissful marriage, but couples must be ready to make efforts to achieve this.

Types of Communication

Let us now look at the types of communication that we must acquire to build effective communication models in our marriages.

For this book, I would list some modes of communication which are more pronounced in marriage, please note that the list is in-exhaustive.

Listening

The number one form of communication is listening. There is a common saying in management that the greatest communication skill is listening. The person who does not listen does not hear and thus does not understand. Effective communication in marriage begins with listening. The reason why you have not be able to find harmony with your spouse is that you have not taken your time to listen to what is being said and also what is not said. A good marriage is a marriage where both spouses take the time and the patience to listen to each other's words, thoughts, inactions and even actions. Couples must learn the art of listening to each other. The reason why your wife shouts at you may be because you have not taken the time to listen to what she is saying and to what she is not saying.

In his book "The Five Love Languages," the author, Gary Chapman did an in-exhaustive study on the five love languages of people and how it applies in the marriage context. I believe that chief among the five languages though not listed as one of the love languages by Chapman, is listening. If one keeps speaking and the person being spoken to, is not listening, whatever is being said and however it is said will be a waste. Effective communication in marriage, therefore, behooves on couples to learn the art of listening.

Verbal Communication

Another form of communication that is worthwhile in marriage is verbal communication. I say this because a lot of spouses assume that couples should know what to do and when to do it. This is not true and should never be given a place in your marriage. There is no place for assumption in marriage, never you think and assume that your spouse knows what to do and hence should do it.

No! Communicate what you want in words or writing and then keep it simple as much as you can. Don't assume; communicate!

Non-verbal Communication
There is of course the place of non-verbal communication which is the third type of communication. In a later chapter, we will talk more about body language which is a type of non-verbal communication. We must seek to understand the body language of our spouse: understand his or her tone of voice, seek to understand his or her facial expression, seek to understand your spouse posture and gestures; and this understanding comes with time, by asking questions and much more, none comes from assumption!

What you don't understand in your spouse, ask him or her, and he or she will tell you as long as you are asking in love and ultimately to find harmony with him or her. Don't forget this; assumption is the mother of frustration (in life and particularly in marriage).

Now that we have looked at the place of communication in marriage and its importance, the question is, what communication model are you going to adopt in your marriage that will achieve the desired result through words or messages? The important thing is to find out what works for you and your spouse. If your spouse is the one who wants to be listened to, then listen to him or her. If your spouse is given to gestures and expressions rather than talking? Then seek to understand his or her body language. Harmony is very important in your home; so at whatever the cost, seek to have such. The dividend on the long run is worthwhile to keep and save your marriage!

Helpful hints in Communication
- Learn to listen to each other
- Do not nag or boast
- Stick to the subject of communication
- Set a timing for serious discussion
- Attack the subject not the person
- Value each other's point of view

CHAPTER TWO
TRUST

The heart of her husband doth safely trust in her, so that he shall have no need of spoil. Proverbs 31:11.

What is Trust?

The Merriam Webster's dictionary among many other definitions, define trust as that which is the ground of confidence, where confidence is a reliance or resting of the mind on the integrity, veracity, justice, friendship, or sound principle of another person. Now let us look at it more closely, the marriage relationship is the strongest and closest of all relationships and it is as strong as our relationship with God through Jesus Christ. We don't see God yet we believe that He lives, exists, and does things because of what we have learned, read, and believed through Scriptures in the Holy Bible. By this, we believe in God with complete reliance and confidence because of what we have read about Him in the Bible. His word, which is the Holy Scripture, gives us the basis for believing. The word of God is His bond, and by that word, we believe and have faith in the integrity and responsiveness of God. Is it any wonder that the Scripture talks so much about our relationship with God as though with a husband and a wife? We are even likened and proposed by Scripture as being married to God!

Trust in marriage

Trust is another component that can either make or ruin a marriage. Where there is trust, there is peace; where there is peace, there is progress, and where there is progress, there is joy, happiness, and fulfillment. But where there is no trust or where trust has been betrayed, there is all manner of issues; ranging from suspicion to accusation and ultimately betrayal and eventually separation if care is not taken.

That said, I want us to turn the spectacle of our mind into our marriage relationship just like we also have with God. The basis of the relationship with your spouse is trust, and the basis of trust is integrity and what defines integrity is the ability to say a thing and to stay and stand by what is said. In matters of integrity, your word is your bond, and your word is you. The Holy Scriptures talk about a person who swears to his hurt, that such a person can be trusted, who knows the place of integrity.

He that sweareth to his own hurt, and changeth not. Psalm 15:4b.

Do you talk about building a relationship with people, particularly with your spouse? How did that relationship all start out? It started with your husband professing his love to you. All you had were his words (what he said), you believed him and stepped out on those words to build a relationship that has culminated into marriage. So, the building block of your relationship has been words. But what happens the day you find out that all your husband or wife had said of himself or herself were all lies and falsehood? Trust and confidence will be eroded. So it is important that couples tell themselves the truth, at all times and especially from the beginning of the relationship.

The Bedrock of every Relationship

Relationship; every form of relationship and particularly the marriage relationship rises and falls on TRUST. When it is taken away, things will fall apart because the center (TRUST) can no longer hold. But like every other ingredient that makes for a successful marriage, trust has to be earned and worked at over time with all the necessary adjustment that we can muster in the process.

...and they lived happily ever after?

It may happen that you have not been entirely sincere to each other during your courtship. You may have secrets such as having a child out of wedlock or been married before or any other undisclosed secrets before the wedding, but now that the marriage has been consummated, it is time to set the record straight which of course will take conscious efforts on the part of the couple. The truth of the matter is that nothing hidden is truly hidden. You may need to apologize to each other about so many things in a bid to put the record straight. Don't forget that what you are looking for is trust and integrity in the home and these may not be achieved if the issues that were hitherto hidden are not brought out to the open, treated and laid to rest as though they never were. Keeping secrets is one of the greatest things that destroy marriages.

Confess your faults one to another, and pray one for another, that ye may be healed. James 5:16a.

It is better that truths are told before heading to the altar. However what happens when undisclosed secrets are revealed in the course of the marriage? Can the marriage still be salvaged? Yes, it can! However, to do so, you have to rebuild the trust as stated above through the process of confession, contrition, and forgiveness.

Trust is Earned
Like so many other things that can be earned, trust also can be earned in marriage. With time, as both parties in the marriage begin to open up their hearts to one another, the virtue called trust will take its place at the center of the marriage. As the spouses begin to work at building their trust gauge, in no time, it will be full and earned, and you can

be sure that when it is earned, it will not be eroded by whatever circumstances that may arise. When that happens, you can vouch for each other any day, anytime, and come what may. Please earn your trust with your spouse, it is not automatic. It is just as the saying goes; forgiveness is free, but trust is earned.

What If Trust is lacking?
There is no substitute for TRUST in your marriage, and you cannot afford the harm it can do to your marriage. So if trust is lacking, there is a need to do a re-appraisal of the entire relationship before and after marriage with the objective to address the issues responsible for the lack of trust. After that couples can resolve to build a marriage on the foundation of TRUST with the one all-sufficient ingredient of TRUTH by telling the truth at all times no matter how much it hurts.

Trust is redeemable; it can be restored where it has been lost, as long as both parties are willing to tell themselves the truth. Satan is adept at deception, and he will work at making sure that you do not have peace and harmony in your home. He will make you feel proud to admit your wrongs, and what you do not admit to, you do not take responsibility for and consequently do not repent or change from such. No one should be bigger than the marriage; when it comes to choosing between your marriage and your ego, your marriage should take priority. Adjust a hundred times if need be, be sorry a hundred times if that is what is needed to build trust and integrity in your marriage.

Helpful hints in Trust
- Trust is earned, so make efforts to earn your spouse's trust
- Be sincere, honest and open to each other
- Do not make assumptions, rather discuss issues to ensure clarity
- Avoid situations where your trust could be compromised
- Do not jump to conclusions

CHAPTER THREE
FINANCE

Be careful for nothing; but in everything by prayer and supplication with thanksgiving let your requests be made known unto God. Philippians 4:6.

Does Money Matter?

The most basic things in life revolve around money; food, clothing, and shelter. It is important to mention that 30% to 40% of issues encountered in marriages are money- related. It takes money to do a lot of things such as pay bills, provides food, shelter, clothing and other essentials things that make for the smooth running of day to day marital life. It may be well for you to say that love does not pay bills but money does. After the marriage has been consummated, the reality of life and the function of money is clear, and adjustments that have to be made are clearer.

It is needless to say money is very important in marriage, but sadly most people have misconceptions about money. While some people believe that money is not an issue in marriage, some believe that money is all that matters. I will talk about these two misconceptions.

It is wrong to think that money is not an issue in marriage. The bible tells us that if a man wants to build a house, he must first count the cost before he commences the project. The same is true for a man who wishes to go into marriage; you must first count the cost by ensuring that you have the finance to provide the basic things in life; food, shelter, and clothing for both you and your spouse. The woman, on the other hand, must also be able to stand as the help-meet for the husband. Please do not get me wrong, I'm not saying that you should have millions in the bank for marriage to happen, all I'm saying is that couples should have enough to start a life. The basic thing is that the couple must have means of livelihood before they go into marriage. Some people may not agree with me on this, yes certainly there are cases of couples going into marriage with only the man having a means of living or only the woman having a means of living. I must tell you that these two cases come with their challenges. However it is more on the later than on the former, and if care is not taken, such marriages may hit the rocks.

I will illustrate the above my own personal experience. My husband and I got married a few months after he lost his job. We were already planning to get married before this happened and my husband felt the marriage should go on in spite of this. Friends, I can tell you that the few months into the marriage during which my husband did not have a job were quite challenging for both of us, with emphasis on my own part. However, with our faith in God, the love we share, the vows we made and our commitment to the marriage, we were able to weather the storm. The situation is a bit bearable with only the husband having a job. However, there are also challenges as the wife will have to depend on the husband for both her needs and that of the house. This may create a financial strain on the husband, and the related stress may cause problems in the marriage.

On the other hand, there are people who believe money is everything in marriage. They quote the Scripture:

...but money answereth all things. Ecclesiastes 10:19b.

Yes indeed, money answers all things, but it's not about everything. A man who plans to acquire much wealth before going into marriage, stand the risk of a lady marrying him for his wealth and not for love. A lady who plans to marry for wealth will also stand the risk of not getting sincere love from the man who will always have this question at the back of his mind; 'would she have married me without my wealth'? Please do not get me wrong ladies, it is not wrong to marry a wealthy man, however, please do not let the only standard for marriage be based on wealth, rather marry for love and other virtues you desire in a man, and let wealth be a bonus!

Running the Home

I make bold to say that the running of the home is 70% to 90% dependent on the woman and this is achieved with money. This is where the wisdom of the woman comes in as written in the Scriptures:

Through wisdom is an house builded; and by understanding it is established. Proverbs 24:3.

There is a belief that the joy, pride, and fulfillment of a man is in the pursuit and achievement of his dreams, vision, and goals, while that of a woman is with her family. If you open up a man's heart, what you will see is his business, goals, vision and how to make money. However, for the woman, you will find the husband, children, and thereafter career, business, relatives, friends, and others as women are generally caring by nature (my apologies to the men). But how will she cope if she does not have knowledge of fund management? How will she achieve her objectives if she does not have financial intelligence? So for the woman, here is the question: how much of financial intelligence do you have? The best you can be for your husband is to be able to manage his scarce resources judiciously. I tell you the truth; every man wants a woman that can manage his money for him wisely as written in the scriptures:

The heart of her husband doth safely trust in her, so that he shall have no need of spoil. Proverbs 31:11.

The day your husband finds you a good manager of funds then you may have just won another part of his heart! There is no man that would not love a woman who can run the house with the fund given to her by the husband and even have a little to put away in savings.

Let us get down to the basics: the wife is the financial manager of the home and therefore has to learn to take care of the home in an economical way and even make a profit from it for the good of the family. Besides more often than not, the money given by husbands for the upkeep of the home may be inadequate, so at such times the wife is faced with minimal resources against a multitude of needs to be met. It is the knowledge of economics and market intelligence that will help in this situation. So if possible, you may need to take time to learn or read about fund management to equip you with knowledge on what to do when you are faced with limited resources against large expenses. What better ways to solve the problem than prioritizing and cutting down on frivolities and excesses that can be done without.

Living within your Means
After the wedding, couples should be left alone by family members to allow them build their homes and fend for themselves without interference. If the husband is wealthy or from a wealthy family, there will be no issue in providing for the family. However on the contrary, if the wife is from a wealthy family, and comes with a mindset to maintain her standard of living in her marital home, especially in a situation where the husband is not financially strong, such mindsets, will surely create issues in the home.

A man who has an ego to protect will stop the wife from taking from her family. This is to prove to her that he can provide for his family without external assistance. The pride of every genuine husband is to be able to take care of his wife without the help and interference of an external body, particularly the family of the wife. In the light of this truth, what are you going to do to protect the ego of your husband who apparently doesn't have enough! I tell you what; you have to learn **Money Management!**

Managing Money

Money is something that should be managed. It is liquid; it has value and is measurable. To successfully run the home and meet up with family expenses, money must be handled with care and pre-planned for, before it comes and disbursed appropriately the moment it lands on the table. I am sometimes taken aback by some women who seem not to understand that not all money should be spent, but rather some should be put into an investment. Particularly in this time of global economic downtime, the skill and knowledge of money management are highly priced by individual and corporate bodies. The family will be well off for it if they learn it.

Money is not to be lavished frivolously on things that are supposedly important unless they are planned for. It is not advisable to spend money that is not planned for when such money comes, it should be put aside and reserved until there is a genuine need for it, or better still it should be saved or invested.

From the preceding, we can see that money matters in marriage and wisdom on the path of the couple is crucial to its allocation and utilization.

It is important to know the financial capability of the family and stay within the budget. This would involve cutting cost, prioritizing, adjusting your taste, staying disciplined and be ready to make sacrifices.

Financial Transparency and Accountability
Before we wind up the chapter, we should look at the role of financial transparency and accountability between couples. I've heard stories of wives who have issues with their husband requesting to give account of funds received for home expenses. It is obvious that such wives are not financially transparent and as such do not want to be accountable. There is nothing wrong in giving an account of how funds given to a wife by the husband is expended. Your husband must trust you with money. If you are accountable, he will trust you with more, believing that you are a good fund manager that can be trusted to utilize the funds for the good of the family judiciously.

Money is important, and it is not always enough. It should, therefore, be handled with wisdom, understanding, and transparency. We cannot shy away from money matters as it can tear the family apart as much as sex matters. It is one of the major instruments that turn the engine of the family, so it's best to be wise and be ready to make the necessary adjustment to ensure a home where the financial crisis is not a frequent occurrence.

Helpful hints on Finance

- Have faith and trust in your husband's ability to provide for you and the family.
- Be a good steward of what your husband can provide.
- Learn to be creative in the ways you find to have your needs and wants, and those of your family met.
- Learn to be the appreciative and supportive helpmate God intended you to be to your husband.
- Provide your family with the necessary things for their upkeep as much as you are able.

CHAPTER FOUR
COMMITMENT

What therefore God hath joined together, let not man put asunder. Mark 10:9.

The Commitment to Love

The words obligation, responsibility, and loyalty are words that are synonymous with commitment. I believe we can relate to these terms. Marriage puts an obligation on the husband and the wife. They are obligated to God to keep the sanctity of the marriage. A husband is obligated to love his wife and provide for the home while the wife is obligated to respect the husband to take care of the home. In the quest to understand the meaning of commitment, I realized that commitment is love. Love is more than just erotic feelings, attraction, and affection, but is also commitment and responsibility. You have to love someone to be able commit yourself to that person. Couples need to understand this and approach marriage in a more understanding way.

Commitment in Marriage

The issue of commitment and responsibility has to be settled in your marriage, and it is crucial for you and your spouse to sit down and to talk it over. The day you say "I do" to your spouse, is the day you become each other's responsibility and priority in all your undertakings. Parents and other family members should automatically take second place. The wife is the priority of the husband, and likewise, the husband is that of the wife.

Furthermore, it is important to know that commitment is both in word and in deeds. Your word must be your bond, the marriage vow is first and foremost a commitment to words by which couples must commit to each other in the course of their marriage. The marital vow *"till death do us part"* is a commitment that couples must commit to as long as they both live.

There may be times and seasons in the course of your marriage where other things and people, particular employers of labor will ask more from you. However, the responsibility is on you to know that any call or commitment that comes at the expense of your marriage is not worth it on the long run. You will eventually realize that your marriage is more important than your job anyway. I do not mean to say that you should quit your job, but if by any chance you are faced with such a challenge, you will have to seek a solution and adjust accordingly and prayerfully.

The Force of Marriage
There is no potency in marriage except that given to it by commitment. It is the enduring decision to see that your marriage works that which will make it work. It is also that decision that will fuel it and keep it going when tough times arise. I charge you to commit yourself to do all that is righteously possible to make sure your marriage works. It is this commitment that will eventually see you through on the long run. The quote by Maya

Angelou, an author that, "nothing works except that which is worked" is also true for marriage.

Marriages are failing today more than ever before in the history of the world. The devil is on a rampage and is doing all that is within his power to fight and to bring down marriages. Your commitment to protecting your marriage will empower you to frustrate the wiles of the enemy. I would like for you and your spouse to intermittently remind yourselves of your marital vows and then tell yourselves that you are in this for the long run. It is that simple! When you do this, the power of your spoken words will work for you and with God on your side, you can be sure that you will win in your marriage.

Sustained through Commitment
What started by commitment, groomed by commitment must also be sustained by commitment. This is true of everything in marriage and much more. As the days roll by into months, months turn into years and youthfulness turn into maturity, the commitment to sustain the marriage should also grow stronger with time. This is necessary because issues may arise in a marriage

that were not part of the original plan, and when these issues occur, it will take the sustained renewed commitment to keep the marriage going. If issues such as loss of a job or terminal ailment arise, what do you do? This is when you recall your marital vow of *"in sickness..."* and a renewed sense of commitment should evolve. The decision to commit to your spouse irrespective of whatever circumstances that may arise, will sustain you in the days of the storm.

Face it and Live it

You may have heard the phrase *"face it or leave it"* but I would say *"face it and live it"*.

Marriage is hard work but pleasurable, marriage is good, but it has its down times. It can sometimes be uncertain and unpredictable, but it takes the tough, the strong and the committed to making it work. Face it and live it, you will have challenging times in your marriage, but you also have the power to overcome if you know what you are supposed to know and do what you are supposed to do. That which you are supposed to know and do begins with the commitment to know and to do. Are you prepared to work on your marriage?

There is a saying that "marriage is a school that one never graduates from". This means that we keep learning and adjusting *until death does the parting*" prayerfully in our old and grey years. There is also another saying that marriage is the only institution where you are given a certificate before you begin. Every other institution will allow you go through the process of learning and afterwards award you a certificate of academic achievement. The marriage institution is however different, you are awarded a certificate with all the courses and subjects in the waiting for you to pass. Now, this is hard work, but it can be done!

Helpful Hints on Commitment

- Resolve in your hearts to be committed to each other
- Be patient and bear with each other in love
- Create time for yourselves to do things you both enjoy

- Love at all times even in tough times!

CHAPTER FIVE
ROMANCE

Let him kiss me with the kisses of his mouth: for thy love is better than wine. Song of Solomon 1:2.

The Romance Flavor

If romance is said to drive the life of a marriage, then a good understanding of how much it means to each party is important. The husband may either be high on romance or the wife, the important thing is for the couple to discuss and adjust accordingly to have the best romance in their marriage.

I'd like to mention here that romance and sex are two separate activities. Romance is the sensitive way of showing love to your spouse while sex is an act. Romance may lead to sex, while sex can be performed without romance. However, in marriage, the two should work together to make a whole. There is a saying that women enjoy romance more than the sexual act, while men enjoy the sexual act more than romance. While this may be true to an extent as women are known to enjoy romance as a prelude to the sexual act, it does not necessarily mean they do not enjoy sex. A woman will enjoy sex with her spouse if he is patient enough to carry her along and ensure she also enjoys the sexual act as much as he does. A wife who does not enjoy sex with her spouse will always feel reluctant to engage in the act. Couples, therefore, have to discuss and agree on what gives them pleasure and ensure commitment to such accordingly.

Keep the Fire Burning
One of the ways to keep the marriage going is for couples to keep the flame of romance burning in every possible way they can. You may want to take your mind back to when you were dating and the fire of love that burned in your hearts. What about the anticipation to get married and live together as husband and wife. Is the fire of love still burning in your hearts? Or have you both settled down to the reality of life where the demands and pressure of work hardly allow you time to spend with each other?

Sometimes couples allow the romantic feelings to grow cool over time after the wedding. Are you still giving yourselves to shared experiences to stimulate affection and appreciation? Our understanding of the relationship that God has with His children is a direct correlation to the relationship of marriage. Without this spiritual understanding, it is difficult to understand the concept of marriage as a union that allows married couples to make the necessary sacrifice to fulfill each other's needs. The same way God cares, comforts and meet our needs is the same way couples should care, comfort, and meet each other's needs.

Let me tell you however that as challenging as the pressure of life may be, it is very important to ensure that the fire of your romance is kept burning and not neglected or relegated to the background. The reasonable fact is that; a neglect of romance and sex will eventually lead to marital problems. It is therefore important for couples to understand this and make adjustments to prevent such a scenario. The fire of romance must be kept burning, a lot depends on it!

Body Language

This is a non-verbal communication between two people, however in this context it is intimate. Couples in a bid to seek to understand and maintain the romance in their marriage must understand each other's body language. The greatest frustration comes from miscommunication in this respect.

Romance is much of a body language than it is for verbal or oral communication. The gestures and the advances of the parties must be studied, understood and responded to, at all times. Again like every other thing that makes for marriage, this aspect must be worked at carefully and dutifully. Do you know your husband's sex language? Do you know your wife's signal for romance or sex?

Emotional Intimacy

Emotional intimacy includes touching, caressing, hugging and kissing. There are millions of touch receptors in the human body, with more than two million in the hands alone according to a BBC Science and Nature documentary. Studies have shown that touching releases feelings of pleasure and healing in both the touched and the touchee. Women are known to love emotional intimacy, and without the elements of intimacy mentioned above, sex with a woman is a likened to a domestic rape!

Wives don't forget that you will get what you give! You will be accepted, appreciated, and affectionately acknowledged as you are genuinely willing to accept, appreciate and acknowledge your husband. I believe we get what we give; it is no coincidence, every action precipitates an equal and opposite reaction. It is very important for couples to show affection to each other at every opportunity they get. They can hold hands while walking together, a touch or a pat on the shoulder and a kiss often.

Sex

Sex is a very important aspect of romance, and sadly most people go into marriage with some misconceptions which has resulted in broken marriages. There is a misconception that women should not be the initiator of sex in marriage as they may be labeled as promiscuous. This situation is very challenging for the wife as she may find it difficult to express her feelings to her husband. Husbands should endeavor to encourage their wives to initiate sex as it creates a healthy home. On the flip side, a husband who initiates sex all the time may feel undesirable to the wife. This, of course, may lead to the temptation to seek affection outside the home.

It is important to emphasize again that sexual satisfaction between couples must be discussed and agreed with the intent to seek to satisfy each other. The joy of romance in marriage comes when the husband and the wife go out of their way to learn how to satisfy each other. There is no place in marriage for a selfish lover! Couples should strive to satisfy each other and not self. Your goal is your spouse's satisfaction in everything, in sex as it is in all other aspects. Why not get committed to this goal!

The Giving of your Body

The Bible makes it explicitly clear that in marriage, the bodies of couples no longer belong to them individually. To the husband, the wife has right and power over his body, and to the woman, the husband has right and power over her body. There is no place for holding back, and there is nothing like "my own or your own." Your body belongs to your husband, and your husband's body belongs to you.

I'd like to ask you this question as we close this chapter: do you still see your body as your own or as belonging to your spouse?

Helpful hints in Romance
- Profess your love to each other as often as you can
- Be affectionate to each other
- Go out on dates as often as you can

- Surprise each other with occasional gifts
- Seek to satisfy each other in the sexual act and engage in it as much as you can

CHAPTER SIX
LOVE

God provides us with a definition of love. 1 Corinthians 13.

The Unconditional Love

Love according to Merriam-Webster is defined as a feel of strong or constant affection for a person. However, love is usually associated only with the eros type of love also known as erotic love. It is based on feelings of attraction associated with sexual desire or romantic relationships. This kind of love is based on physical attraction and it can be selfish and possessive and usually does not last except when it is redeemed by God. The other two types of love are the philos and agape. Philos love is the type of love that exist between a mother and child, brother and sister, and friends and it is characterized by shared experiences. This is also the type of love that exists among Christians. The agape love on the other hand is the divine love of God to all creation. It is the best of type of love because it is unconditional and does not depend on feelings. Agape love is the love God commanded for all believers to have for everyone whether they are believers or not.

⁴Charity suffereth long, and is kind; charity envieth not; charity vaunteth not itself, is not puffed up, ⁵Doth not behave itself unseemly, seeketh not her own, is not easily provoked, thinketh no evil; ⁶Rejoiceth not in iniquity, but rejoiceth in the truth; ⁷Beareth all things, believeth all things, hopeth all things, endureth all things, ⁸Charity never faileth:…1 Corinthians 13:4-8a.

This puts a whole new perspective on the meaning of the words, "I love you"!! Consider for a moment what this type of love looks like. "Honey, I love you. What I mean is I am patient and kind with you. I do not envy you; I do not boast in front of you, I am not proud before you. I am not rude to you, I seek your good and not my own, I am not easily angered by you, and I keep no record of your wrongs." Wow! If only we could love like this all the time!

Love in Marriage
If we are honest, however, most of us will admit that this type of love is not always easy. Part of

the reason for this is that we find it easier to be selfish than to be selfless. It is far easier for us to think only of our needs rather than the needs of our spouse. When we love this way, the tendency is for the spouse not to feel truly loved.

One of the primary characteristics of godly love, however, is that it is focused more on others than ourselves. The above scripture says "love is not self-seeking" and indeed Jesus in the scripture below says,

Greater love hath no man than this, that a man lay down his life for his friends. John 15:13.

This, of course, is exactly the type of love that Jesus has for us, and the type He expects us to share with our spouse. How do we learn to love like this in our **marriage**?

Understanding the difference between Passionate and Companionate love
The experience of 'being in love' involves an intense and unrealistic emotional reaction to another person, also referred to as *passionate*

love. At such times, we may see our loved one inaccurately, i.e. we may see them as "perfect" in every way, emphasizing their virtues and dismissing their faults as unimportant. However, passionate love is too intense and unrealistic to be maintained in a permanent emotional state.

Other kinds of love that can be long lasting such as *Companionate love,* which is described as the love that is based on friendship, mutual attraction, shared interests, respect and concern for one another's welfare. It may not seem as exciting as passionate love but it is a crucial aspect of a satisfying and lasting relationship.

Since many of us mistakenly equate only romantic feelings or passionate love with love; in long-term relationships like marriage, we may begin to wonder what happened to our heady *feelings* of love. Living together involves doing numerous house-hold chores, paying bills, finishing to-do lists or going to work. None of these are particularly known to inspire feelings of romance or passionate love between people! Yet it is these very activities, done together that forge strong bonds of deep caring and attachment, also known as companionate or mature love. Companionate love is based on a better understanding of ourselves and our partner.

How Love grows in a Marriage
Love is the magic potion of long-term relationships. Love grows from knowing and sharing with our partners. For example, if a husband and wife go out on a date, they may not necessarily feel an intense emotional reaction as they experienced in the 'in love' or passionate love stage. Instead, they may enjoy the time spent in togetherness and develop

deeper emotional or intellectual intimacy by getting to know more about their partner through their conversation. Thus, our efforts every day to know and share with our partners would lead us to greater levels of physical, emotional, intellectual, financial, recreational, and spiritual intimacy.

To enjoy companionate love in marriage, we may need to get over our hurt and disappointment often brought about by unrealistic or inaccurate beliefs about love. Building intimacy in marriage may require planning our time and efforts. If you would like to explore your own beliefs about love and how these may be impacting you and your relationships or if you would like to understand and identify ways in which you could build intimacy in your marriage, you could talk it over with a counselor. The story below is an illustration of passionate and companionate love.

The story of Josh and Joyce
Josh and Joyce (real names withheld) met in college and fell in love. They dated through college

and after graduation decided to get married. However, there was a problem, as both their parents were against the marriage due to inter-cultural reasons. Josh and Joyce decided to get married secretly at a marriage registry. Both families were angry and disappointed with their action but there was nothing they could do since they were already married.

Five years into the marriage the story was not the same, they both got busy with their careers and consequently drifted apart. When Joyce realized the danger that was lucking in the corner of their marriage, she decided to take up the issue with Josh in an intent to save her marriage from collapse, but Josh who had gotten used to the "status quo", was unwilling to listen, especially since his family members who never approved of the marriage had been trying to get Josh to separate from Joyce.

A distraught Joyce with no one to talk to, resolved to turn to God in prayers. She took time off from work to fast and pray for God's intervention in her marriage. Did God intervene? Oh yes He did! On that faithful day, Josh came home early from work and saw Joyce on her knees crying and praying to God to save their marriage. A touched Josh, with tears in his eyes, went on his knees and joined his wife in prayer. They both cried out to God to save their marriage and had since then continued to pray together as a family and are living happily ever after!

What do you think was responsible for Josh and Joyce drifting apart? The marriage was based on passionate love, and they did not make the efforts to build the companionate love in their marriage.

The story also is a prelude to the subject of the next and concluding chapter of this book; PRAYER!

Helpful hints on Love
- Be kind to one another, love is kind
- Spend quality time together
- Give gifts to each other as you can afford
- Perform acts of service to one another by doing what pleases each other
- Love unconditionally

CHAPTER SEVEN
PRAYER

Again I say unto you, That if two of you shall agree on earth as touching anything that they shall ask, it shall be done for them of my Father which is in heaven. Matthew 18:19.

Prayer changes everything

Prayer is the act of communicating with God. It is an act of worship and a love relationship. It is simply baring our soul to the One who loves us and allowing Him to speak to our hearts.

I will start this chapter by discouraging new couples from coming into marriage with big expectations about each other and getting upset when such are not met. The changes that you try to bring about in your respective spouses are doomed to fail as it is only God that can bring about such change. You can only pray to God concerning your expectations while you pray together and for each other.

If I may ask; how often do you pray with your spouse? Do you pray for yourself? Do you pray for your marriage? The responses received each time I ask these questions have been quite interesting; while most couples inform they rarely pray together, some felt they do not need to pray with their spouse since they each observe their personal devotion separately, some acknowledge that it is good for couples to pray together but simply fail to put it into action, while some confess they pray together.

Which do you believe? Do you believe prayer is important to your relationship or is it just a ritual you perform? Do you believe that prayer has a huge impact on the depth of companionship in your marriage? In reality, what you *do* at present in your home is the clearest revelation of what you believe regarding prayer. Prayer is the binding force that holds together all the essentials of marriage that have been discussed above. Without prayer, it would all have been fruitless efforts and charade.

The family, principally a husband and wife living together in peace and harmony, is the smallest unit in a society. A strong family produces a strong society and likewise a weak or troubled family produces same. The current situation in the society speaks of the state of affairs in the family. The devil is always on rampage to destabilize and destroy marriages, hence couples must therefore perform the act of praying together daily in order to withstand the wiles of the enemy. My husband and

I adopted this attitude quite early in our marriage, and 25 years later and still counting by God's grace, we are still praying together!

The following discussions elucidate the benefits of prayer as a building block in marriages.

Prayer unites us spiritually before God
One of the greatest reasons God wants couples to pray together is as illustrated in the scripture;

...That if two of you shall agree on earth as touching anything that they shall ask, it shall be done for them of my Father which is in heaven. Matthew 18:19.

Prayer naturally brings you into an agreement with one another as you hold your petitions before the Lord. You can't pray whole-heartedly and in a unified manner without agreeing together. By coming before God you are naturally uniting your hearts to one common end. This unity was the fruit of collective prayer in the early church. When the apostles were persecuted, the believers came together and

...when they heard that, they lifted up their voice to God with one accord,...Acts 4:24a

The testimony of the above scripture reveals that when they finished praying together,

...the multitude of them that believed were of one heart and of one soul:...Acts 4:32a

Now is there anything that couples need more than to be of one accord with each other? How different is this attitude from the independence that many couples profess these days? The "one accord" stated in the scripture indicates a depth of relationship that is truly satisfying. If you desire this level of spiritual unity in your marriage, begin to pray together and watch your oneness grow. This is God's design for prayer in marriage.

Prayer encourages Humility and Honesty
Experiencing unity of heart with your mate is not automatic. It requires intent by both spouses. Jesus taught that an honest and humble heart is an absolute essential for effective prayer when He told the story of the two men who came to the Temple to pray. One claimed self-righteousness and ended up praying with only himself because God abhors the prayer of a proud man. The other however humbled himself and cried out,

…God be merciful to me a sinner. Luke 18:13b.

The Bibles tells us that only the prayer of the humble man was accepted and justified before God.

In the same manner, couples who come together in humility and acknowledge their personal needs before God will receive the much-needed grace for their marriage.

One of the marital problems that I observed as a marriage counselor is the refusal of couples to acknowledge their weakness or need to one another which can be resolved through praying together. It is important for couples to be reminded that no one knows each other better than themselves, so a refusal to come together in prayer only keeps you further from one another and the depth of relationship you long for in your marriage. Therefore, when you pray together, be honest and humble yourself before God, confess your needs openly, and be drawn closer together as a result.

Prayer deepens Communication
One of the greatest benefit of couples praying together is that it increases their intimacy and

brings them closer to God. During prayers, couples are able to discover each other's deeper needs which may not have been mentioned or discussed during conversations. They are therefore able to connect and agree with each other on such needs.

A good example is a wife who discovers her husband's needs during prayer, will come to realize the significance of that need to him, and will, therefore be able to further connect with him on that issue. The same is also true for the husband. A commitment to praying together and obedience to God communicates a sense of responsibility between spouses to fulfill their obligations in marriage. Oh, what a sweet fruit of trust and intimacy this will bear! Good communication as elucidated in chapter 1, is fundamental to real companionship and prayer is the hand that turns the key to open this door!

Prayer establishes deeper Companionship
What do you think are the key issues that hinder real companionship with your partner? Is it a sense of independence, pride, and fear or a lack of communication? As couples humbly pray together, communicating their needs before God, they will automatically develop a spiritual bond that results in deeper companionship which is a great aspect of marriage. The book of Malachi specifically made

this clear when it referred to a marriage partner as *"companion" Malachi 2:14.* If you lack companionship in your marriage, prayer is one very important way to deepen it. If couples do not unite together in prayer, there will always be a depth of companionship that will be lacking. Remember, the closer we get to God, the closer we get to each other.

> **" Prayer is opening your heart and life to God to allow Him, in the power of the Holy Spirit, and with Christ to pray in, for and with you.**
>
> **Prayer is what God is doing in your heart."**

Your Marriage will be built up because you will be built up

You will never be the loser by giving yourself to pray with your spouse. The Bible makes it clear that when a believer prays he or she will be built up as a result according to the scripture;

But ye, beloved, building up yourselves on your most holy faith, praying in the Holy Ghost. Jude 1:20.

As you pray and spend time petitioning and communing with the Father, He will build you up. Jesus promised that the Holy Spirit will come to fill your heart because of prayer:

…how much more shall your heavenly Father give the Holy Spirit to them that ask Him? Luke 11:13b.

If you and your spouse are filled with the Holy Spirit, your lives will manifest the fruit of His Spirit, *Galatians 5:22-23,* which is what every marriage needs. As you are built up personally with these qualities, your marriage will also be built up, and your home will be wonderfully strengthened.

Beloved, don't miss out on God's plan in your marriage because of individuality, pride, or fear. *Open your heart and ask the Father to work in you to will and to do of His good pleasure, Philippians 2:13.* You won't be sorry!

Helpful hints in Prayer

- Find a mutually agreeable time.
- Keep to the prayer time
- Pray for your marriage

- Pray for your spouse, children, family members,…
- Pray without ceasing

PRAYER FOR MARRIAGE

Oh Lord, I thank You for our marriage and pray that You would bless and protect it from harm. Shield it from our selfishness, neglect, unhealthy and dangerous situations. Protect it from the evil plans and desires of external forces. Set us free from past hurts, memories, misconceptions, ties from previous relationships, and unrealistic expectations of one another. I pray that there will be no low self-esteem or envy in either of us. Let nothing come into our hearts and habits that might threaten the marriage in any way. Unite us in a bond of Love, Commitment, and Prayer. Eliminate our immaturity, hostility, and feelings of inadequacy. Help us to always make time for each other alone to nurture and renew the marriage and remind ourselves of the reasons we were married in the first place. I pray that we will be committed to You, Lord, and to each other regardless of whatever storms may arise. May there be no thoughts of divorce or infidelity in our hearts and none in our future. I pray that our love for each other will grow stronger and passionate with each day so that we will not leave a legacy of divorce to our children. Amen

To contact the author, please send a mail to meetabiolasoremekun@gmail.com

Please send in your testimony, comments or knowledge gained from reading this book.

Your prayer requests are welcome.

God bless you…

Printed in Great Britain
by Amazon

65377680R00043